PIECES OF A MAN

THE FALL. THE MIRROR. THE RISE.

JAIWAUN T. HAGGERTY

CONTENTS

Dedication

December 10ᵗʰ

"Damn, this is going to be the greatest story ever, I swear on my life. I disappointed everyone, but I know they're going to love this comeback. I'll be an amazing dad, an amazing person, an amazing partner because this major setback is going to be an incredible comeback."

Jay

For the nights I thought I wouldn't make it,
For the mornings I did anyway,
And for anyone who's ever loved so much it hurt.
This is for you.

ACKNOWLEDGEMENT

To the friends who let me talk in circles,

To the strangers who didn't even know they were keeping me going,

To the people who left and the ones who stayed – Thank you for shaping the story I didn't know I was writing.

And to her, your impact will always be felt in these pages, not out of blame, but because you were part of my becoming.

This is for the women in my life I love dearly **Momma and Nana.**

AMFx2

You both have seen me at my lowest
and still believed in my rise.
This book is my apology, my growth,
and my proof that change is real.

The best apology isn't words —
it's actions.
And this book is both.

In loving memory of a woman
who saw the man I could become
and left this world too soon —

Mary Eliza Singleton

Your belief in me still guides my steps.

ABOUT THE AUTHOR

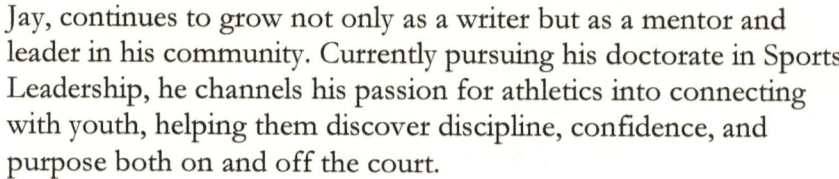

Jay, continues to grow not only as a writer but as a mentor and leader in his community. Currently pursuing his doctorate in Sports Leadership, he channels his passion for athletics into connecting with youth, helping them discover discipline, confidence, and purpose both on and off the court.

Family has always been at the center of Jaiwaun's life. Through every triumph and setback, he has remained close to those he loves, drawing strength and perspective from their shared experiences. A guiding lesson he carries is that "the grass is greener when you water it"—a philosophy that has deepened his friendships and strengthened family bonds alike.

Coaching basketball this year, Jaiwaun has embraced the opportunity to teach more than just the game: teamwork, resilience, and character are as important as every point scored. Watching his friends grow and pursue their own paths inspires him to keep pushing forward in his own journey, balancing ambition with gratitude, and action with reflection.

Whether in the classroom, on the court, or within his personal life, Jaiwaun's story is one of continuous growth, intentional connections, and the pursuit of a meaningful legacy.

PREFACE

I didn't wake up one morning and decide to lose her.

It happened in slow motion, like a crack in glass that keeps spreading no matter how still you try to hold it. One argument turned into three. One mistake turned into something I couldn't take back. And then there was silence.

I started writing because I couldn't talk to her anymore. These pages became my only way to speak without being heard and to bleed without anyone seeing the wound. Every word here is a timestamp, proof that I felt it, lived it, and somehow made it through.

This isn't a story about getting her back. This is the story of how I got myself back.

What Are Mirror Moments?

Throughout this book, you'll find something called a **Mirror Moment** at the end of each chapter. These moments are small reflections, pauses meant for you to look inward and see how my story connects to yours.

When I was healing, I realized that every painful moment was really a mirror showing me who I was and who I still needed to become. These reflections are my way of passing that mirror to you.

Each one begins with a truth, something I learned the hard way, followed by an open question to help you dig into your own experience, and a simple intention to carry forward. There's no right answer, no judgment, and no rush. Just honesty.

Take your time with them. Sit in the silence. Reread them if you need to.

Sometimes the mirror shows you what you lost, but more often, it reveals what you've been carrying all along.

CHAPTER 1 |
THE NIGHT IT ALL FELL APART

"Jay, why do you keep doing this to me?"

Her voice cracked like glass under pressure, sharp enough to cut through the quiet. Tears streaked down her cheeks, each one carrying a piece of something I swore I'd protect. She wasn't screaming, not yet, but her eyes held the kind of rage that makes words dangerous.

We'd been sitting in her room for hours, not really speaking, just arguing in silence, throwing looks sharp enough to wound, shifting in our seats like two people on the edge of a cliff. Her parents were asleep in the next room. It was two or three in the morning, a weeknight. In a few hours, I was supposed to be at work. But the idea of going to bed felt like trying to sleep through a house fire.

You might be wondering what could cause this kind of chaos at this hour. What madness could bring two people who swore they'd spend forever together to this place?

Well, we all know what happens when someone goes through their partner's phone.

They find things.

She found mine.

And what she saw cut her deep. A message thread that didn't belong to her. A name she didn't recognize. A truth she didn't want to believe, especially not with our first engagement anniversary just a day away.

I could see it in her face. The disappointment. The betrayal. The disbelief that the man she trusted with her heart had been sharing pieces of himself with someone else.

And here's the part I can't hide from anymore: everything we had, I risked for nothing. I had the woman, the home, the car, the job, the friends, everything I used to dream about as a kid from the hood. And I threw it away like it was a scratch-off ticket I didn't think would pay out.

Because that's what I learned growing up where I'm from: nothing good lasts. Heat works today; it's gone tomorrow. You get attached to something, and it disappears. So instead of holding onto love, I tested it. Pushed it. Sabotaged it. Broke it before it could break me.

That night, November 10th, wasn't just the night she found out. It was the night I saw myself clearly for the first time, and I didn't like what I saw.

I thought I was protecting myself. But really, I was just teaching myself how to be alone.

After that night, as the house grew colder and the silence pressed down heavier than ever, my mind drifted back to the only place I'd ever known to be somewhat steady, the home of my childhood best friend, J. Black, also known as Jason.

So, I built walls. I pushed people away before they could leave me. I treated love like a set-up because, growing up, love *was* a set-up.

Love has always felt like a set-up for me. Not in a cliché way, but in the way it lifts you, makes you feel safe, then tests you when you least expect it. I learned it first from my mom, who loved me fiercely but whose attention shifted when another man came into her life. I learned it from my older brother, who made me feel invincible until the day the system took him away. DCF stepped in, and visits turned into long drives to group homes, the kind of distance that teaches you how to love someone from afar. I felt it with my dad, my hero, who taught me hard lessons and then left this world too soon. Even with women, I gave my all, time, love, and trust, only to learn that it can fade without warning.

Each time, love built me up, only to knock me down. But every setup came with a lesson. It taught me resilience, empathy, and how to carry my heart carefully but openly. More than anything, it showed me that love isn't just about joy, it's about growth.

And that's what made me love the way I did with her.

That night, after the storm of words and tears, I felt numb, like my emotions had been drained and replaced with a heavy fog. Guilty, confused, but never angry. I knew I had no right to be mad because I was the one who caused the damage.

She had given me a chance, a real chance, to fix things. To stop the cheating, cut all the ties and lies, and love her again like she deserved. But inside me, after six years together and a wedding on the horizon, a dark question gnawed at my soul: *Did I really want this?*

I shut down immediately. Not because I didn't care, but because I didn't know how to face it. I never made her feel like it was her fault, even though she felt the weight of my silence.

I remember holding her tight as she cried, she says, *"Why me? Why do you do this to me? Do you even love me?"* Her words pierced through the numbness I wore like armor. I wanted to scream back that yes, I loved her, but all I could do was hold on tighter.

Work the next day was harder than that night. I made a terrible mistake with someone I knew from an event, and as fate would have it, she also worked at my local supermarket. It was a choice that went against everything I believed about myself, and it hurt not just her but also the people I loved and valued.

The moment I saw her, I felt it immediately, something electric in the air. She had this way of looking at me, like she knew everything, like she could see the line I was walking and still wanted me to cross it. She didn't need to say much; the way she talked, the way she laughed, it was enough to pull me in.

I knew she knew. She knew I was with someone else, and yet that just made the thrill bigger. Every word, every glance, carried that dangerous excitement. My chest tightened, my pulse sped up. I couldn't decide whether to engage or step back, because part of me wanted the rush, and part of me wanted to stay safe.

We talked, but it was more than words; it was the way she made everything feel alive, the way she made me feel like I was breaking the rules in the best possible way. I couldn't help but be drawn to it, to her energy, to the thrill she brought. In that moment, I wasn't thinking about consequences. I was thinking about the fire she lit just by being there, just by knowing exactly what she was doing.

That moment forced me to confront the kind of man I wanted to be, the man I had been failing to show. It was a painful wake-up call, but it became the catalyst for me to take responsibility, reflect deeply, and embark on a journey toward self-improvement. Every moment, her face haunted me. My mind raced with a million thoughts while I stood in line at Big Y, putting on a fake smile and pretending everything was normal.

In my head, the questions never stopped: *Is this the end? Do I want to be with my fiancée? Do I need to hit reset?* Why was I even questioning it when she had been my ideal partner for so long? I was blinded, blinded by lust, a bruised ego, and the reckless belief that I could find something better. I ignored the undeniable truth: I loved this woman deeply.

Physically, the pain was real. My chest felt tight, like it was being squeezed. My heart sank so low it felt like it was pounding against the floor. But emotionally, I was numb, detached from the devastation I was causing both of us. That numbness wasn't just from the fight or the guilt; it came from years of carrying a heavy weight I didn't fully understand back then.

Growing up, I saw love in its rawest forms. My mom raised six kids on her own, loving us fiercely in the only ways she knew, sometimes with warmth, sometimes with silence or anger. She never gave up, but the men in her life often did. They left, they used her, they broke promises. With each goodbye, I learned a truth I couldn't shake: love doesn't always last.

That truth settled deep in my bones. It whispered whenever I got close to something good: *It won't last. It's a set-up. Leave before you're left.*

I carried that fear into every relationship, including the one I was about to lose.

And so, even as she cried and begged for my love, even as my heart broke in silence, my mind kept building walls. I wasn't ready to believe that love could be steady, that it could last, that I deserved it.

I didn't know it then, but that night was more than just the end of a relationship. It was the moment I faced the truth about myself, the fear, the pain, and the walls I'd built to keep love at bay.

Love felt like a set-up because that's what I'd been taught growing up. But deep down, I wanted something different. I wanted to believe love could last.

Because no matter where you come from, no matter how deep the scars, you deserve good things. Especially love.

Mirror Moment:

"The moment everything fell apart was the same moment I started to see myself clearly."

Reflection: What truth did that kind of heartbreak reveal in you that you still haven't said out loud?

Intention: Don't curse the breakdown, sometimes it's your soul demanding to be rebuilt.

CHAPTER 2 |
WHERE THAT FEAR WAS BORN

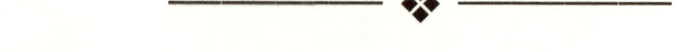

As a kid, the first and fourteenth of every month felt like paydays. Not from a job, welfare and SSI checks kept us afloat, kept the lights on, and put food in the fridge. My mom could stretch a dollar until it begged for mercy. That's what I loved about her: she made magic out of scraps, turned nothing into something, and still found ways to make us smile.

The fourteenth was like Christmas morning. Food stamps hit, and suddenly the cabinets looked like a commercial, name-brand cereal stacked high, Lunchables lined up like little treasures, Scooby-Doo fruit snacks spilling out of their packages, and enough Gushers to fuel me until dinner. But the days in between were a different story.

Nights felt longer, colder, hungrier. Summers pressed down on our apartment like a weight, tempers flaring in the sticky air. That's when Nana came through. She had this sixth sense for when we were running low, bags of food from the church in her arms, Styrofoam trays wrapped in foil, cornbread muffins in plastic bags, sometimes even sweet potato pies that hadn't sold. She'd set them down like laying out gold. In those moments, she made me feel bigger than I was.

We moved a lot, Mission Hill, Dorchester, Mattapan, Hyde Park, Roxbury. Roxbury stuck with me the most. But moving that often taught me that houses were just buildings. Home wasn't a place; it was people. And at the center of that home was my mom. She was my first best friend. She poured love into me like it was oxygen. Even when men mistreated her, mentally, physically, she shielded me from it. She smiled through pain, laughed when she could, and made me feel safe. That love shaped me. It made me a mama's boy, and I'll never apologize for it.

Some of my happiest memories were in the kitchen with her and Nana. The two of them cooking was like church. Nana at the counter, seasoning meat heavy-handed, telling stories "from back in the day." My mom blasting Mary J. Blige so loud the walls vibrated, hitting every note like her life depended on it. On other days, it was Earth, Wind & Fire, Anita Baker, The Gap Band, and Luther Vandross. Those records made me an old soul before I even knew it.

The kitchen smelled like life itself, collard greens simmering, honey butter cornbread rising in the oven, fried chicken popping in hot oil. Metal spoons scraped cast iron, my mom shuffled between stove and sink, and Nana laughed, telling her to "stir that pot like you mean it."

Moving boxes stacked in the corner reminded us we wouldn't be there long. But in those hours, just the three of us, the world outside didn't exist. That's where I learned comfort. That's where I learned connection. That's where I learned that love could be tasted, smelled, and heard.

Love, though, has always been a double-edged sword. On one side, it was a blanket of safety, like walking through the grocery store with my mom's hand in mine, her laughing as I tried to sneak a box of Watermelon Gushers. That laughter made me feel untouchable. But love also left me exposed. When a man came into her life, the warmth they had slipped away. My older brother's disappearance into a group home taught me that people you love can vanish overnight. My dad's kidney failure showed me that even the strongest figures can be gone before you're ready.

My older brother showed me the thrill of brotherly love, the hidden streets of the city, sneaking out, breaking rules, and feeling invincible. And then he was gone, sent away because of his behavior. That first taste of abandonment left a mark. Even love that seems solid can disappear overnight.

My baby brother, Jaivonni, gave me another side of love: protective, tender, fragile. He looks up to me in a way that makes me feel responsible and accountable. Loving him taught me that the weight of love is both a blessing and a responsibility, and letting someone down, even accidentally, hurts like losing them entirely.

Then there's my dad. Aaron Jean Haggerty. My hero, my mentor, my guide. He loved me, yes, but he was human, flawed, stubborn, selfish at times. He struggled, he cheated, and eventually, kidney failure took him from me. Losing him was the ultimate set-up: love came strong and guiding, then it left, leaving me to carry the lessons he had given me, to fill the gaps his absence created, and to try to be a better person than he was.

And love wasn't just about family; it was also about exes. My first serious girlfriend made me feel like I could be understood, like someone really saw me. I gave her everything, time, trust, loyalty, but she left in ways that stung deep. Small betrayals, broken promises, faded affection, they all taught me that even when love feels safe, it can quietly prepare you for heartbreak. Another set-up.

With my ex, it was different. We laughed, argued, loved, and fought through life's chaos together. But I learned that love doesn't always protect you from selfishness, neglect, or misaligned priorities. You can give your all, and yet the other person's love can falter, leaving you to question yourself and the meaning of what you shared. Each heartbreak reminded me that love is both a gift and a challenge.

Love has always been a setup for me. At least, that's what it felt like. Real, deep love, the kind that lifts you, then tests you, leaving you exposed. I've felt it with my family, my exes, and those I thought were supposed to love me unconditionally. Through all of it, I've learned that love comes with both joy and lessons you aren't ready for.

Even in moments of happiness, love set me up. It made me vulnerable, raw, and exposed to disappointment. But it also made me human. It taught me resilience, empathy, and self-awareness. I learned to carry my heart carefully, but openly. Love isn't just about joy; it's about growth, understanding people and their limits, surviving when the warmth fades, and standing on your own.

Looking back, I see a pattern: love lifts me, challenges me, leaves me, and teaches me. Family, exes, friends, they all set me up in their own way. But through every setup, heartbreak, and lesson, I've grown. I've learned what it means to love fiercely, to endure, to rise stronger. And now, when I love, I do it with intention, wisdom, and an understanding that love will always challenge me, but it will also make me who I am meant to be.

Mirror Moment:

"The things we fear most often trace back to the love that failed us first."

Reflection: When did you first start expecting pain in places that were supposed to be safe?

Intention: Healing begins when you stop confusing survival with love.

CHAPTER 3 |
THE FIRST LOVE I
COULDN'T HANDLE

❖

Coming from a home where my mom and Nana poured everything into me, I thought I understood what love was. I thought I knew how to receive it, and I thought receiving it was enough. But when I met her, my first serious love in high school, I learned there's a big difference between *being loved* and *knowing how to love someone back*.

At first, it was the kind of relationship people dream about in their teenage years. She was smart, warm (sometimes), and carried herself with a confidence that made me feel like I had made the right choice. We were together for four years, and on the outside, it looked solid. But inside? It was heavy with pride and ego. We both had this unspoken attitude that we could walk away at any time and be fine, yet we kept coming back to each other. That push-and-pull became our normal.

It wasn't all bad. We had fun. We made memories. We had moments where we felt unstoppable. But deep down, I think we both knew we didn't feel safe enough to be vulnerable with each other. And for me, that became a pattern. Whenever things got hard, even just a tough conversation, I would shut down completely. If it was uncomfortable for me to talk about, it wasn't going to happen. That habit was like a slow leak in a tire; it didn't blow up overnight, but eventually, it wore the relationship down.

I didn't realize it at the time, but I was already showing signs of self-sabotage. I would "test" her to see how far she would go to keep me around. I'd let my pride tell me that *I* was the prize and that if she couldn't handle me, someone else would. I sought validation from other women, not always physically, but even having certain conversations was crossing a line. I didn't understand that once you break someone's trust, even just through talking, you've already planted a wound that might never heal.

The Second Chance at Love

When I entered my second serious relationship, this time as a young adult in college, I thought I was ready. I convinced myself I had matured, that I knew what I wanted, and that I wouldn't repeat the same mistakes. I had taken time to be single, but even then, I didn't really know where to begin. The real question I avoided asking myself was: *Who did I need to become for my next partner?*

And in many ways, this relationship was completely different. She loved me in a way I had never been loved before, deeply, fully, without conditions. She rooted for me when I didn't even believe in myself. She showed me that real love wasn't just words; it was actions, affection, encouragement, and unwavering support.

It was hard for me to accept that kind of love at first. Not because I didn't want it, but because I didn't know how to *receive* it without ruining it. I was so used to chaos that peace felt unnatural. And instead of leaning into that love, I let fear and ego creep back in.

Part of why I struggled in that relationship wasn't just me; it was the patterns I carried with me from growing up. When I felt insecure or overwhelmed, I didn't know how to talk about it. I pulled away, shut down, and left no room for her to share her own feelings. That silence wasn't random; it came from years of learning that vulnerability wasn't always safe. As a kid, emotions were heavy, messy, and sometimes unwelcome. I learned to protect myself by holding them in.

In my weakest moments, I sought attention from other women, not because I didn't love her, but because that outside thrill fed my ego. Love had always been confusing for me. I'd seen it as comfort, yes, but also as a set-up, something fragile that could disappear at any moment. I chased the temporary proof that I mattered, even when it conflicted with the deep love I already had for her.

The hardest truth I've had to face is this: I hurt someone who loved me at my lowest, someone who chose to stand by me even when I gave her every reason not to. And while my actions were mine alone, the roots of that behavior trace back to lessons I never fully unlearned, the lessons that taught me how to survive, but not always how to love.

The Breaking Point

The specific moment everything started to crumble was when she found out I had been talking to other women again. This wasn't a one-time mistake; it had happened multiple times. Every time, she took me back. And every time, my ego inflated a little more, telling me I must really be "the catch" if she loved me enough to stay through that.

But what I didn't see was the damage I was doing to her spirit. Every message, every conversation, every time I crossed that line, I chipped away at the trust we had built. And once trust is broken, no matter how much love remains, it's never quite the same.

The truth? I was selfish. I wanted to love her, but I also wanted the attention and validation from others. And in chasing both, I lost the one person who truly saw me for who I was and still believed I could be better.

Looking back, both of my serious relationships taught me more about myself than I could have learned on my own. My high school relationship taught me that love without vulnerability can turn into a power struggle. My adult relationship showed me that love without self-awareness and respect is destined to collapse.

I wish I could say I learned all these lessons in time to save us, but I didn't. What I can say is that losing her forced me to face myself for the first time, and that's where the real story begins.

Mirror Moment:

"Love isn't supposed to feel like carrying both hearts on your back."

Reflection:

Who have you been trying to rescue just so you didn't have to rescue yourself?

Intention:

Love that drains you isn't love, it's proof you've forgotten your own worth.

CHAPTER 4 |
A MONSTER WITH
LOVER BOY TENDENCIES

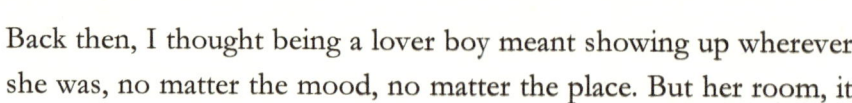

Back then, I thought being a lover boy meant showing up wherever she was, no matter the mood, no matter the place. But her room, it wasn't just four walls. It carried her silence, her weight, her battles.

Her room used to feel heavy. The kind of heavy where even silence pressed against you. She was in a dark season; she'd just lost her job, and it showed in her space. The walls looked tired, her childhood bed took up too much room, the blankets were worn thin, and there was a bookcase still sitting in the corner waiting to be put together, like it had been forgotten. Every time I walked in, I could feel the weight on her shoulders sitting inside those four walls.

So, one day, I decided I wasn't going to let her come home to that anymore. I didn't have much, just a few dollars to my name, but I stretched it into a plan. I tore down that old childhood bed and replaced it with a sleek bedroom set, fresh blankets, new pillows, and sheets that made the whole room look alive again. I built her that bookcase she'd been waiting too long to see standing. I even set up a computer desk and chair so she'd have a place to study, to dream again.

When she walked in from hanging out with her friends, I stood back and just watched. Her face lit up in a way I'll never forget. That room wasn't just furniture; it was proof that I was willing to flip the world upside down just to make her happy. That's what love felt like to me back then: doing whatever I could, however small or crazy, to put light back in her life.

And it wasn't just the room. Sometimes it was the spontaneous nights where I'd say, "Let's go to Boston," with no bags packed, no plan. We'd hit the road, shop for clothes, grab dinner, get our favorite ice cream, then crash in a cozy hotel room where we'd binge our shows and laugh like we didn't have a single worry. That was our thing, turning ordinary nights into memories.

If I'm being real, the first person who ever taught me how to love was my momma. She was the type of woman who showed love in ways you could feel without her even saying it. The way she cared, the way she made sure I was safe, the way she did the little things, that stuck with me. From her, I learned that love isn't about the loudest gestures; it's about consistency. It's about making sure somebody knows you got them no matter what.

That foundation carried over into the way I loved women. I naturally became caring and genuine because I grew up watching my momma give that kind of love. That's why, when I got older, I knew how to rub her feet after a long day, how to cook dinner and have it ready, how to surprise a woman with flowers or small things that reminded me of her. That came from home. That came from being raised around unconditional love.

But here's where it gets tricky: loving like that doesn't mean you always know how to protect someone's heart. See, I had this woman, and I loved her in ways I didn't even know I could. I'm talking that 90s love, singing to her, holding her, making sure she felt good around me. I loved doing those things because it made me feel like she was safe in my arms. That was my highlight seeing her smile because of something simple I did.

At the same time, I have to be honest with myself. As much love as I gave, I was selfish too. I loved her so much that sometimes I cared more about my own pleasures than her well-being. And that's where the contradiction came in. On one hand, I was the man rubbing her feet, buying flowers, and being spontaneous. On the other hand, I was the same man who betrayed her trust. That's not easy to admit, but it's the truth.

And here's the thing, I don't say all this to make myself sound like a monster or to play victim either. I was a good man in a lot of ways, but I messed up in the most important one: protecting her heart. That's something I had to learn the hard way.

What that relationship taught me, though, was how to love deeper. My momma gave me the basics: how to care, how to provide, how to be thoughtful. But she, this woman, taught me that love is also about sacrifice, about truly putting somebody else's heart before your own. She showed me that love ain't just about comfort, it's about growth.

And that's where the lesson lies. Fellas, listen to me: making your woman feel safe in all aspects is everything. I'm not just talking about money or gifts. I'm talking about your presence. Your consistency. Your honesty. Get to know her. Learn her. Study the small things, because they matter. If she likes her coffee a certain way, learn it. If she gets anxious in certain spaces, notice it. If she lights up when you do something small, repeat it. It's always the little things.

At the end of the day, love is about making somebody feel like they can exhale when they're with you. That's what my momma gave me growing up, and that's what she taught me to give. I just had to realize that part of making someone feel safe also means protecting them from your own demons.

So yeah, my momma taught me how to love. But she taught me how to love deeper. Together, those lessons shaped the man I'm still becoming. I just had to stumble, fall, and face myself to finally understand what real love requires.

Mirror Moment:

"Sometimes the villain in your story wears the same face as your comfort."

Reflection: What signs did you silence because you didn't want to lose what felt familiar?

Intention: Believe what people show you the first time, not the version you build in your mind.

CHAPTER 5 | ROCK BOTTOM IN THE DRIVER'S SEAT

When I realized I still loved her, it hit me like a brick to the chest. The breakup wasn't just the end of a relationship; it was the loss of my home, my safe place, the future I had imagined. We had been living together, trying to make a life under the same roof, while she also had her own place. She didn't want to put me out, but the level of disrespect was too much. I know it hurt her to make that choice, and that thought still twists my stomach.

Even after I knew I wasn't in my right mind, I took the cheating further than ever. I can't fully explain why. Part of me was numb. Part of me was angry. And part of me just didn't care enough about myself, or about her, to stop hurting the person I loved.

Once it was truly over, the numbness faded, and the full weight of it hit me. Life went from sharing a room, dreaming of a future together, to sleeping in my car for three weeks. December 1st. My birthday. I spent it in Boston, numb but alive for a few hours, out with Ashley and Alexia.

Laughter, music, distractions, the kind of night that covers pain like a thin blanket. But the next morning came. Work didn't care it was my birthday, didn't care my relationship was over, didn't care I hadn't slept. I drove to my mom's house, showered, and told her I was staying at a hotel. She believed me. Everyone believed me. My friends thought I was with my mom. My mom thought I was in a room somewhere safe. Nobody knew where I really went.

When the sun dropped, I headed to the same parking lot a mile and a half from my job. Not home, not even close. Just a strip of asphalt tucked between Big Y and Dollar Tree. The kind of place nobody would look twice at. For three weeks, that became my address.

I picked it for convenience, close enough to work so I could wake up, wipe the sleep from my face, and be there on time. At night, I hit Planet Fitness, not to lift but to shower, hoping the steam could wash off more than just the dirt. Then back to the car.

The back seat was small, barely enough room to curl up. Little to no blankets. The December cold snuck in through the cracked windows and stiffened my joints. I'd tuck my hoodie under my head, fold my arms across my chest, and try to trick my body into believing it was safe to rest.

But it never felt safe. No Benji at my feet. No woman beside me. Just silence, broken by the occasional slam of a car door or the rattle of a shopping cart.

Lying there, shivering, I asked myself over and over: *Who's listening right now? My dad? God? Both?*

I didn't get an answer. Just a reminder that this was my life now. This was my consequence.

I had messed up everything. My home. My relationship. The future I thought I had. And now it was just me, this car, and a December night that didn't care if I made it to morning.

Still, every night I pulled out my phone and typed. Poured out the guilt, the regret, the loneliness. Because if I didn't, the silence would eat me alive. Writing in that car was my only proof I still existed.

This was the exact moment I wrote these words in my phone, on December 10th:

Journal Entry, December 10th

Damn, this is going to be the greatest story ever, I swear on my life. I disappointed everyone, but I know they're going to love this comeback. I'll be an amazing dad, an amazing person, an amazing partner because this major setback is going to be an incredible comeback.

That's what I held on to. In that car, freezing, alone, abandoned hope was the only blanket I had left.

Middle of December…cold nights, lonely, my breath fogging in the air as I tried to sleep. That transition happened too fast. I was hurt, ashamed, and above all, I felt undeserving of love, not because she didn't love me anymore, but because I no longer felt I deserved anyone's love.

Those nights in the car were the quietest, loneliest nights of my life. Just me, the cold, and the constant replay of my mistakes. I'd stare at the roof above me, thinking about all the times I could have done the right thing, and every single time, the same conclusion came: it wasn't worth it.

Looking back, most times, and especially in this moment, I was lying to myself. I wrote about being ready to let go, about healing, about not overthinking anymore, but deep down, I wasn't there yet. I still wanted answers, I still wanted her, and I was still clinging to hope. I see now that writing these words was part of me *trying* to believe them, even if I hadn't fully caught up emotionally. It was less about where I truly was and more about where I wanted to be.

Something had to give. I couldn't keep living like that, mentally or physically. On December 4th, I signed up for therapy and a gym membership on the same day. I knew I needed to change emotionally and physically.

At first, I didn't tell anyone. I kept it quiet, only sharing with four friends, Ashley, Alexia, Jean, and Manny. I was scared they'd look at me differently. But they did what real friends do: they called me out for what I did, told me how wrong I was, and still showed up for me because they knew I wasn't beyond redemption. That kind of love and accountability is rare, and I'll never stop being grateful for them.

Therapy was a turning point. I realized how much men, especially men of color, need to talk more about their feelings, their past, and the wounds they've been carrying in silence. That silence destroys us. I had been carrying so much that I never let out, and it was bleeding into every relationship I had.

Facing the Mirror

I remember that moment in her office like it was burned into my chest. My therapist, calm but unflinching, made me say it out loud: *the truth about my love and my ego.*

"I loved her," I said first, my voice tight, shaky. "More than I've ever loved anyone. She was my anchor, my home. Everything I wanted to protect, to honor, to keep safe."

She leaned in slightly, letting the words hang. "And yet?"

"And yet…" I swallowed hard. My chest felt tight, like it was being crushed from the inside. "I chased attention from other women. I sought excitement that wasn't love. It fed my ego, my need to feel wanted, alive, in control. It was reckless. It was selfish. And it hurt her."

Her eyes stayed on me, steady. "Can you *feel* that?" she asked. "Not just understand it in your head, but feel the weight of it?"

I did. Every memory of her face, every argument, every silence, every moment I failed, hit me at once. Shame settled in my stomach like concrete, heavy and immovable. My heart raced, my hands shook. I wanted to shrink into myself, disappear from that moment. But I couldn't. I had to stay.

Then, slowly, something shifted. Relief began to seep in, not the relief of escaping blame, but the relief of truth. I could finally see it, finally name it: love is patient, enduring, building. Ego is fleeting, impulsive, and destructive. Love wanted me to stay, to honor her, to grow. Ego wanted me to run, to chase, to break. And I had been trying to serve both, and in doing so, I had hurt the one I loved most.

I closed my eyes and let it all in, the shame, the regret, the love, the pain. And then I opened them and whispered to myself, not out loud but in the stillness of that office, "I see you. I know now. I have to be better."

It wasn't sudden. It wasn't cinematic. There was no lightning bolt or grand revelation. But it was real. And for the first time, I felt determination replace the chaos. I felt the possibility of being a man who loved fully, honestly, without letting ego rule. That night, I walked out of her office lighter than I had in years, carrying accountability like a shield, not as punishment, but as armor for the man I was determined to become.

Through therapy, I had to accept some hard truths: I was a cheater. I was controlling. I was addicted to sex. I was egotistical. Saying it out loud made me feel like I didn't deserve love at all. But naming it was the first step to changing it. Jason Wilson once said, "The greatest downfall of a man is lust." Sitting there in that office, I realized that downfall had been mine. Lust made me believe I was in control, when really it controlled me. It wasn't just about women; it was about ego, validation, and the undisciplined parts of me that wanted the easy thrill instead of the steady work of love. Therapy forced me to see that clearly: lust is a trap, and discipline is the only way out.

The only setback came when I'd see my ex, and we'd have a moment where it felt like maybe we could get back together. That hope was dangerous. I don't believe in "no contact" as some sort of secret path back into a relationship. Once it's over, it's over. Get yourself together for you, not for them, because it might not work out, no matter how much you love them.

Crash Out Moment

Some men have one. Some men need one. Mine came like a strike of lightning, on Juneteenth, in the middle of a Miami party. The kind of party where the bass shakes your chest, lights strobe across sweaty faces, and laughter ricochets off the walls, but in that moment, none of it mattered. All I could see was her. After months of silence, distance, and heartbreak, there she was.

The moment our eyes met, something inside me snapped. My chest tightened, my heart hammered like it was trying to escape my body, and before I knew it, I flipped out. She saw me, but she didn't respond. She protected her peace. Ignored me. I thought she was baiting me, trying to push me, but the truth was brutal: she couldn't emotionally engage. Her walls were up. Mine were crumbling.

I said things I never thought I would. Words I'd regret instantly. I mentioned having someone else, but the reality was, I didn't. "That's why I found better," I blurted, though I hadn't given anyone a chance because I was still healing. I wanted to hurt her. To lash out at the pain inside me. But the chaos was uncontrollable. I wasn't myself that night.

The rooftop air was thick with heat and tension. The Miami skyline glimmered behind us, a million lights reflecting my inner turmoil. You would have thought the party kept going, but no.

The music slowed. Conversations hushed. The energy shifted, like the universe itself had paused for this moment. My pulse thundered in my ears. Security hovered near her, asking if she was okay. Her lips didn't speak, but her tears did, shining in the strobe lights.

I ended up back with my friends, but outside the party, under the humid Miami night sky, the heat still pressing down, the sounds of the city distant, I felt the weight of everything I'd done. My heart raced, my chest burned, and regret was a living thing crawling inside me.

Some men have a "Crash Out Moment." Mine arrived like this: sudden, blinding, unavoidable. That night was raw. It was real. It tested me in ways I wasn't prepared for. And while I wanted to lash out, I couldn't. It reminded me how easy it is to give someone else power over your emotions, and how critical it is to take that power back. Pain became fuel. Anger became motivation. Mistakes became lessons.

Juneteenth in Miami wasn't just a party; it was a wake-up call. A fiery, uncomfortable, humbling reminder that growth doesn't start when things are easy. It starts in the heat of the hardest moments. That night marked a turning point: I realized I couldn't let my emotions dictate my actions anymore. I had to let them guide me toward the man I knew I could become.

Mirror Moment:

"Rock bottom doesn't destroy you, it introduces you to your truth."

Reflection: What had to break for you to finally see who you really were beneath the weight?

Intention: The fall was the foundation, not the finish line.

Chapter 6 |
What I Couldn't Say:
A Letter of Advice to the
Woman Who Loved Me

This is written as a letter to her, the woman who loved me at my worst, who carried the weight I wasn't strong enough to hold. But it's not just for her, it's for anyone who has ever loved a man like me. If you find yourself in a relationship where he pushes you away, sabotages what could've been good, or hides behind pride, I hope these words speak to you, too.

When I reflect on my actions, I see a man silently crying for help. Most of the time, my behavior wasn't about her; it was about my own battles, insecurities, and mistakes I hadn't yet faced. I pushed her away, avoided confrontation, and hid behind my pride, making her question what she was worth. She could support me, love me, even guide me, but she couldn't fix me. And the hardest truth? Sometimes the only way someone like me can grow is to step back, reflect, and experience the consequences of their own actions.

Most times, and at that time in particular, I was lying to myself. I told myself I was fine, that I had control, that I was handling everything, but deep down, I was struggling. I was avoiding the truth of my own behavior and pain, convincing myself that avoidance was strength. It wasn't. It was a weakness. The lesson? Don't lie to yourself. Face your reality, own your mistakes, and take responsibility. That's where true growth begins.

That's why our breakup became necessary. Painful? Absolutely. But transformative? Without a doubt. I needed that space to become a better man, to learn to love myself, understand my pain without letting it define me, and turn the foundations of my mistakes into lessons for growth. I had to confront my own demons: my fear of commitment, my pride, my self-sabotage. And I had to do it alone. For anyone reading this, here's what you need to remember:

- **Support, but don't enable.** Encourage growth, honesty, and reflection, but never cover up repeated mistakes. Your love is powerful, but it has limits.

- **Boundaries protect you.** If he refuses to see his flaws, resists change, or continues harmful patterns, stepping back is not giving up; it's necessary for both of you to grow.

- **Watch actions, not words.** Apologies and promises mean little without consistent, tangible change. True transformation is visible, not just spoken.

- **Step back when needed.** Love sometimes means letting go, even temporarily. It's painful, but it allows him to rebuild, take responsibility, and truly grow.

- **Value yourself.** Never let someone else's struggles diminish your worth. Your patience and guidance are gifts, they're not obligations.

I know firsthand how hard it is to love someone like me. My choices hurt deeply. I caused confusion, pain, and heartbreak. But through it all, I learned that real change comes from within. I had to face my flaws head-on, confront my patterns, and make conscious choices to grow. Only then could I begin to love fully, communicate honestly, and respect the person who loved me.

I've spent most of my life learning the hard way what love really means. Growing up, I watched relationships come and go around me, some built on genuine connection, others on control, fear, or the excitement of chaos. I saw my parents, my friends, and even myself stumble through patterns that left people hurt and hearts bruised. And slowly, I realized that love isn't just about feeling, it's about showing up, even when it's uncomfortable.

What I've come to understand, through years of mistakes and heartbreak, is that a full love package isn't a fantasy; it's a reflection of what I wish I had and what I learned I needed to give. It's about emotional connection, being present, vulnerable, and genuinely understanding another person. It's about trust, believing in each other's integrity and intentions. Respect, honoring boundaries and individuality. Shared values that guide life and decisions. Physical attraction, compatibility, a willingness to grow together, open communication, and the commitment to navigate challenges as a team.

I didn't always understand this. When I was younger, I equated intensity with love. I thought desire and attention could fill the gaps left by my own insecurities. But I learned that love without respect, without real emotional availability, doesn't last. It can feel consuming, addictive even, but it won't sustain you. Real love demands showing up every day, listening when it's hard, apologizing when you're wrong, and confronting your own shortcomings before blaming anyone else.

I can trace much of my struggle back to my childhood. Growing up in a neighborhood where survival sometimes meant putting ego over empathy, I learned to protect myself, to hide my vulnerability, and to sabotage what felt too close or too risky. Those lessons worked for a time, but in love, they became obstacles. Loving someone like me isn't enough to fix me. It takes patience, encouragement, and understanding, but it also requires me to take responsibility for my actions. And sometimes, the only way to grow is to be left alone with your mistakes long enough to see them clearly.

That's what my breakup taught me. It forced me to look in the mirror, confront my patterns, and finally begin building the man I wanted to be. Love is beautiful, but it's not always enough. The full package only works when both people are willing to show up fully, even when it's hard, even when past mistakes weigh heavy. When it works, when both people commit to growth, respect, and consistency, love becomes rare. It becomes lasting.

This isn't just a confession. It's a reflection of my life, the choices I've made, and the lessons I've learned through heartbreak, growth, and self-discovery. I've hurt. I've hidden. I've sabotaged. And through it all, I've begun to understand what it means to love and be loved fully.

Take care of yourself. Encourage growth. Protect your heart. And know this: sometimes, the greatest act of love is letting go so someone, including yourself, can finally become who they were meant to be.

Mirror Moment:

"Sometimes forgiveness isn't for them, it's the release that frees you."

Reflection: What apology still lives in your chest, heavy and unspoken?

Intention: Speak your truth, even if it never reaches the person you broke. Healing doesn't wait for permission.

CHAPTER 7 |
BUILDING A NEW LEGACY: LOVE, HEALING, AND GROWTH

This fall from everything I thought I had, didn't break me; it changed me.

I'm not just telling my story for me. I want other men, especially men of color, to hear what self-sabotage can do before it takes everything from you.

Cheating? It's never okay. If you're chasing validation, then be single. Don't hurt the people who truly love you. And fellas, therapy isn't just for when you hit rock bottom. It's a tool for releasing the weight you've been carrying for years, the pain, the anger, the confusion. Talking to someone changed how I carry mine, and it can change how you carry yours.

When I'm ready to love again, and I will be ready, I'll love differently. I'll love every day, not just on the good days but especially more on the hard days. I'll be there when my partner's world feels like it's falling apart, because love is a safe space. It's a refuge where no one should ever feel alone.

Stronger Bonds, Real Connections

This journey brought me closer to my friends than I ever imagined. Even when miles separated us, their love, honesty, and unwavering presence never faded. Ashley, Alexia, Manny, Jean, Maronel, Emely, Big Y aka Yusef and 2G, these aren't just names; they are lifelines. They reminded me of who I truly am when I was ready to lose myself in doubt, regret, or self-sabotage.

They didn't sugarcoat anything. When I was spiraling, they called me out. When I celebrated small wins, they celebrated as if it were monumental. They held me accountable for my choices, challenged me to be better, and reminded me that growth isn't always comfortable, but it's necessary. No "yes men" allowed, just real love, tough truths, and relentless support.

Even in moments when I felt isolated, they were there. Texts, calls, or simple check-ins became anchors in turbulent days. Their authenticity taught me the value of loyalty, the power of honesty, and that true friendship isn't about convenience, it's about showing up, even when it's hard. They reminded me that I could rise, stand tall, and keep moving forward, not just for myself, but for the people who truly see me.

A Work in Progress

I've made a lot of decisions in my life. Some were mistakes, moments where I acted impulsively, hurt someone I loved, or let my emotions get the better of me. Others were poor choices, decisions I knew weren't right, but I went with them anyway because of fear, pride, or stubbornness. The difference is subtle, but it's real: a mistake is often a surprise, a misstep in the moment; a poor choice is something you already knew could go wrong, and you did it anyway.

I remember one night vividly, a turning point that still echoes in me. I was young, reckless in love, and I let my pride control me. I lashed out at someone I cared about because I didn't know how to process my own pain. That was a mistake. I didn't intend to hurt anyone; I just didn't know a better way to show my emotions. The regret from that stayed with me, gnawed at me, taught me that how I act in the heat of the moment matters.

Then there were the poor choices. Like staying in relationships that I knew weren't healthy, chasing validation from people who didn't have my best interests at heart, or ignoring red flags because I wanted things to be easier than they were. Those are the decisions that haunt you differently. You can't blame the moment; you chose it. You knew better. The regret is heavier because it comes with responsibility. You own it.

It took years for me to recognize the difference. Mistakes can teach you; poor choices demand accountability. And knowing the difference is what shapes the man I've become. It's why I learned to pause before I speak, to evaluate my intentions, and to confront the parts of myself that want the easy way out, even when it hurts.

Looking back now, I don't just see pain, I see lessons. I see the way regret, in all its forms, has molded me. And I know that part of growing up, part of learning to love fully, is being honest about both the mistakes and the poor choices, taking ownership, and allowing yourself to become better because of them, not trapped by them.

I'm still healing. I'm still growing. Healing isn't a quick fix, and it's definitely not a straight line; it's messy, confusing, and full of ups and downs. There are days when I feel like I've taken ten steps forward, and then suddenly I'm hit with a memory, a thought, or a feeling that drags me back. But I've learned that doesn't mean I'm failing, it just means I'm human.

I've spent too much of my life pretending like I was okay when I wasn't, putting up walls, and choosing silence because it felt safer than letting people see the real me. But silence only eats at you.

Now, I'm starting to ask for help when I need it. I see my therapist every week, my feet up on the couch, and just talking about all my issues with the world. I'm learning that vulnerability doesn't mean weakness; it's actually a sign of strength. It's uncomfortable as hell sometimes, but it's the only way to grow.

And the truth is, most times, even in moments like this, I was lying to myself. Telling myself I was fine, that I could carry it all alone, when deep down I was breaking. Do not do that. **Hiding from your own truth only delays your healing.** If there's one thing I'm finally realizing, it's that I can't keep running from myself.

Taking Care of Me, Inside and Out

I learned that healing isn't just emotional, it's spiritual and physical too. Prayer and conversations with God became my daily lifelines. When I felt like breaking down, I'd remind myself of the saying: *"God's favorites have the toughest battles."* That reminder carried me through some of my darkest moments. And now, looking back, I see proof, I'm still here, still standing, still breathing, still moving forward.

Music grounds me in ways nothing else can. Gospel feeds my soul, soul music heals my heart, and old-school jams remind me of my roots, of who I really am.

Each song is like medicine, helping me feel, release, and remember. I've made peace with fully experiencing my emotions instead of running from them. I don't let them control me anymore, but I also don't deny them. That shift created a safe space inside of me, one that no one can take away. And that safe space feels powerful.

Mirror Moment:

"You can't build something new on top of pain you refuse to face."

Reflection: What new standard are you building now that you finally know your worth?

Intention: Let love become your discipline, not your downfall.

CHAPTER 8 |
LETTER TO YOU...NGER SELF

Dear Jay,

This is for the boy who tried to be a man before he had the chance
to just be a kid.
The one who smiled through pain, who learned early that silence
was safer than speaking.
The one who didn't know yet that the same streets that toughened
him would one day inspire him.

You've been carrying weight you never asked for.
You've been trying to protect everyone else before learning how to
protect yourself.
But you made it here—and that alone makes you special.

You were never weak for crying.
You were never soft for caring.
And you were never lost for not knowing who you were yet.

You thought manhood meant having money, women, validation,
and respect from the crowd.
But real manhood came the night you had nothing—when you slept
in that cold car, breath fogging the window, and still promised
yourself you'd make it out.
That was manhood. That was faith.

You'll break hearts, and yours will break too.
You'll lie, you'll cheat, you'll lose people you thought would never
leave.
You'll chase love that wasn't ready for you and run from the love

that was.

But through every mistake, you'll find grace—and grace will find you.

You'll meet God not in a church, but in a mirror.

He'll speak through your lowest moments—when you're tired of pretending, tired of running, and ready to face the truth of who you've become.

And when you do, Jay, don't look away. That reflection will save you.

You'll learn that your anger was never strength—it was pain with nowhere to go.

That your pride wasn't confidence—it was fear dressed up in designer.

And that lust will promise you freedom, but discipline will give you peace.

Lust will take everything you've built if you let it. It'll dress destruction up as desire.

But discipline—that quiet, steady voice inside you—is what will keep your soul clean when the world tries to pull you apart.

There will be nights when temptation feels louder than reason.

When that old voice whispers, *"Just one more time,"* you'll want to listen. Don't.

Every time you trade peace for pleasure, you lose a piece of yourself.

The thrill fades. The emptiness stays.

So walk away. Breathe. Pray.

Every "no" you say to what's wrong is a "yes" to your future.

Love yourself first.

Not in a selfish way, but in a steady way—the kind of love that doesn't beg to be seen, that doesn't need applause to feel real.

The kind of love that allows you to show up for others without losing yourself.

Forgive your father.

Forgive your mother for the things she couldn't protect you from.

Forgive the boy who thought chaos was love.
And when forgiveness feels too heavy, start with understanding.
Because healing doesn't mean forgetting—it means choosing not to let pain control you anymore.

Keep your circle small but honest.
The ones who call you out will save your soul more than the ones who only cheer.
Hold on to your purpose, even when you can't see the full picture yet.
The dream isn't dead—it's just developing patience.

When the world tries to make you forget who you are, remember this:
You come from women who turned nothing into something.
You come from men who fell but got back up.
You come from legacy.

And when anger creeps back in, don't hold it like it's armor.
Let it push you, not poison you.
Build from it. Let it sharpen your focus, not harden your heart.
Because peace built from pain lasts longer than revenge built from ego.

You'll face more storms, Jay.
You'll lose people you thought were permanent, and you'll question if you're enough.
But every trial will teach you something the easy days never could.
Hard times aren't punishment—they're preparation.
God breaks you down only to rebuild you stronger.

So promise me this—
Promise to lead with patience, to love slow, to forgive quickly, and to walk with discipline.
Promise to protect your name, your peace, your heart, and your purpose.
Promise to stay rooted even when the world moves fast.
Promise to keep chasing growth instead of validation.

And when you look in the mirror, ask yourself:
• Am I becoming the man I prayed to be?
• Are my actions worthy of the love I want?
• What choices am I making today that will shape my tomorrow?

If you don't like the answers, change them. Right there. Right then. Because that's what real men do—they correct, they grow, they rise again.

So keep going, Jay.
Keep showing up.
Keep turning pain into purpose and lessons into legacy.

Because one day, you'll write it all down.
And some lost boy—just like you—will read these words and finally believe he can rise too.

With love, truth, and peace,
You.

Mirror Moment:

"The man I am had to meet the boy I was before either of us could heal."

Reflection: What would you tell that younger version of you about the love he was chasing?

Intention: Give that boy the grace you never got, he did the best he could with what he knew.

CHAPTER 9 |
TURNING THE PAGE

❖

I close this chapter of my life with her peacefully. Our love will always exist—but in a different form. She served a purpose, and though it caused pain, it shaped who I am today. Writing this book wasn't just for her—it was for the world. It's the story of reclaiming myself, rising stronger, and becoming more than I ever imagined.

The breakthrough began the moment I boarded that plane to Medellín. It deepened when I took full accountability. And it exploded into release the moment I put my words on paper. Writing didn't just capture my story—it spoke back. It told me to keep going, to let it all out, to be heard.

So thank you—for the memories I'll never forget, for the love that still has a place in me, and for being part of the rebirth of the man you'd be proud of. Letting go doesn't have to hurt—it can be growth, clarity, and freedom.

In the months of no contact, I started in anger. My heart was closed. I refused to feel. But over time, the anger softened, and healing began. I found love again—not with someone else, but within myself. I realized that while I cared deeply, I had to protect myself from the darker parts of me that had been running the show.

Therapy revealed him: the version of me that sabotaged everything I loved. He destroyed relationships, opportunities, and even parts of my soul—all because he wanted to be seen. But now he is silent. He is fading. And soon, he will be gone.

I stand stronger now. My home feels complete—it's just me and Benji, growing, moving, living. I hike more. I run more. I play more with friends across the globe, but in a healthy way. I teach at a school where the community embraces me, where the kids look up to me. I do it for them. I push forward with my education, my doctorate, my dream of becoming an athletic director, and my love of coaching basketball.

Life feels full—like I've been reborn. I'll travel again before 2025 ends. And most importantly, I know I can love again. Until my queen arrives, I'll keep building this empire brick by brick.

As for us—you and I—I've released you. Not from my mind, not from my heart—you'll always be there—but from my soul. The tie is broken. That intimacy we shared, that connection—I didn't know how to honor it then. But we are no longer the same people. We are strangers in the best way—reborn versions of ourselves.

I loved you as hard as I could, and one day I won't love you at all. That's okay. Because I grew, many women may want this man, but only one will earn my forever.

This Jay is new. Improved. God-fearing. Purpose-driven. Free.

And to you, the reader: you are not your past. Storms will come, but they make the sunny days shine brighter. Take control. Make a difference today. Don't wait for tomorrow.

I started over, and so can you. New home. New job. Better friendships. Stronger coping skills. Lighter shoulders. No hate. No bad blood. Just love.

We tried, it didn't work, but it shaped us. Now it's peace, respect, and a quiet understanding. Go be great. Make me proud—I know you will.

This season has been about growth, about learning to open myself again. I've made mistakes, faced setbacks, questioned myself—but every step has forged the man I am becoming. Vulnerability isn't weakness. It's the doorway to connection—with others, and with yourself.

I don't know exactly what the future holds. But I know I'm stepping into it with clarity, purpose, and a heart ready for what comes next. This is the beginning of a new chapter—one I hope inspires others to embrace change, trust the process, and move forward.

I never wrote this book to chase the past—I wrote it to confront the truth and claim my future. Every page became a mirror I couldn't look away from, and every chapter forced me to face the man I once tried to bury. In the process, I rebuilt what I broke, I made peace with my shadows, and I learned that rock bottom isn't where life ends—it's where transformation begins.

This is not a story of heartbreak. It's a story of becoming whole. A story of truth, accountability, and rebirth. I carried pain, but I forged it into purpose. I carried shame, but I refined it into strength. I carried failure, but I reshaped it into fuel. And in the end, I carried words—and turned them into this book.

I leave these pages not with regret, but with clarity. Not with excuses, but with accountability. And not with bitterness, but with the unshakable understanding that everything I lost led me closer to the man I was always meant to be.

If there's anything this journey has proven, it's this: redemption isn't found in someone else's hands—it's found in your own.

If these pages spark even one man to go to therapy, apologize with honesty, or simply believe he deserves love without sabotage—then every sleepless night, every tear, and every word was worth it.

This story began with heartbreak. It ends with healing.

I didn't get her back.

I got myself back.

And that was enough.

Love was never a setup—it was the setup for who I was meant to become.

Mirror Moment:

"The hardest stories to tell are often the ones that set us free."

Reflection: What truth is still sitting in silence, waiting for your voice to give it peace?

Intention: Your pain can't heal in silence, speak it, own it, release it.

CHAPTER 10 |
SOUNDTRACK TO MY HEALING

When words failed me, music spoke. Every song here played when the silence got too heavy, when I was rebuilding myself piece by piece. This isn't just a playlist—it's the soundtrack of my healing, my proof that pain can still make something beautiful.

Intro / Prologue:
• **Dearly Beloved – Wale**
The calm before the storm. A reflection before the rebirth. This song felt like a letter to the man I used to be—a reminder that love, loss, and purpose are all part of the same journey.

• **Men in Black – Will Smith**
The theme song to my book. The energy and confidence set the tone—like stepping into the world fully present, fully me.

Early Struggles (Breakup Shock / December – January):
• **Pain – Future**
The darkest nights in the gym were fueled by this track. The breakup pain found a voice in these beats, turning heartbreak into motivation.

• **A Thin Line Between Love and Hate – H-Town**
Love can lift you, then cut you open in the same breath. This track reminded me how fast something beautiful can turn brutal.

• **All I Got Is You – Ghostface Killah (feat. Mary J. Blige)**
I felt every word. Sleeping in my car, praying through the cold—this song mirrored my survival when everything else fell apart. It

reminded me that even with nothing, I still had faith, family, and breath.

Spiritual Grounding & Discipline (February – March):
• Looking For – Kirk Franklin
God was with me the whole way; I just hadn't acknowledged Him. This song reminded me that I was never walking alone.

• Change You – Babyface Ray
The pain I endured wasn't punishment—it was preparation. I needed this heartbreak to transform me into a better man.

• Mud – Giveon
Slow, soulful, and heavy. I was knee-deep in mistakes, but still fighting to stand. Growth doesn't come clean—it comes from the mud.

• Rain Down – Daniel Caesar
Cleansing, surrendering. This song felt like a prayer for peace, a washing away of everything I couldn't control.

Turning Point (Spring – Gaining Confidence):
• 05:47 – Baby Money
I was just warming up, scratching the surface of what I could achieve. The song reminds me that growth takes time.

• Turned Your Back – Gunna
Betrayal, even self-inflicted, fueled my hustle. Pain can be the strongest motivator.

• Showed Em – Gunna
Proving to myself that I could rise. Quiet confidence. No explanations, just elevation.

• Ambitious Girl – Wale
Ambition, drive, and seeing more for myself. A reminder that growth comes from action, not comfort.

• Who Dat – J. Cole
That spark of self-belief returning. A reintroduction to the man I was always meant to become.

Travel & Freedom (Colombia Trip / Reset Chapter):
• Flights Booked – Drake
My first solo trip. Letting go felt foreign at first, but freedom found me 3,000 miles away. This song captured that release.

• Lost in the World – Kanye West
First time traveling without her. I felt alive, free, and connected again. This song captured the liberation of that experience.

• Just Fine – Mary J. Blige
My mom played this when she felt free from toxic relationships. It reminded me that I, too, could survive, reclaim my joy, and move forward.

• I Wonder – Kanye West
A mirror moment in motion. Questioning purpose, chasing peace, realizing freedom isn't running away—it's returning to yourself.

Rebuilding & Leveling Up (Summer – Self-Discovery):
• Deserve to Win – Payroll Giovanni
The mindset shift. No more guilt—just grind. I was earning back my name, my respect, and my peace.

• Hustler's Ambition – 50 Cent
Grinding day and night to leave my car behind and secure my apartment. Hustle became survival.

• God Gave Me Style – 50 Cent
Blessed and grateful. Realizing I could smile through struggles and appreciate life, no matter what.

• I Can Tell – Giveon
Honest reflection. Learning to express what I feel instead of hiding behind what I show.

• **Damn – Bryson Tiller**
The aftermath. Looking back on what broke me—but without bitterness. Just acceptance, peace, and understanding.

• **Boyz II Men – New Edition**
The perfect anthem for growth. I was evolving into a stronger, wiser man worthy of love and respect.

Victory & Legacy (Reflection / Purpose):
• **Back to Life – Soul II Soul**
The comeback anthem. Returning to myself, grounded in purpose, ready for whatever comes next.

• **Beautiful Bliss – Wale (feat. J. Cole)**
Morning motivation. Even through pain, this song reminded me that storms are temporary and that healing is real.

• **Legacy – Babyface Ray**
Overcoming odds, refusing to give up, and building something greater than myself. A declaration of purpose.

• **Unforgettable – Drake**
I want to be remembered—not just for mistakes, but for the man I became through them.

• **Sky's the Limit – Notorious B.I.G.**
No ceilings, no boundaries. Survival, healing, and transformation— it all made me limitless.

• **Champain – NoCap**
Closing track: untouchable. From heartbreak to healing to purpose, this song embodies the confidence I built through it all.

Each song was a prayer I didn't know how to say out loud.
Together, they became the rhythm of my rebirth—the moment the noise quieted, and I finally heard myself again.

Mirror Moment:

"Every scar sings a song, if you listen closely, it's survival in harmony."

Reflection: What song plays in your soul now that pain no longer writes the lyrics?

Intention: Let your scars be proof that love didn't end you, it evolved you.

Chapter 11 |
The Waves of Healing,
December 8th to June 25th

These words became my heartbeat through the storm. Some days, I could barely write a sentence; other days, I couldn't stop. What you're about to read isn't edited for perfection—it's life in its rawest form. The typos, the pauses, the unfiltered emotion—they're all part of the truth. I wanted you to feel what I felt in real time—the breakdowns, the breakthroughs, and the quiet moments in between. This isn't a polished version of me—it's the proof that I lived, learned, and refused to stay silent.

Words from Jean

"What I'm about to say to you is coming from a brother-to-brother place. I have to be real and honest with you about everything.

First and foremost, I appreciate you opening up to me about what happened. That takes a lot of courage, and it shows that you're reflecting on your actions, which is the first step toward growth.

Taking accountability and responsibility is the hardest but first step you're gonna have to take and admit to of healing. Mind you, I'm speaking from experience, I'm not gonna tell shit just because... telling you all this cause I want this relationship with you two to work, and lastly, you're my dawg and don't want you failing in any aspect of life. I want to be real with you, though, because if you're serious about winning her back, it's going to take more than just apologizing or saying you'll change.

You need to commit to rebuilding trust, which isn't just about words—it's about consistent actions over time. This isn't just about her seeing you as different; it's about you genuinely becoming the best version of yourself. That means:

- *Changing your mindset. Take a hard look at the patterns and behaviors that led to this. What made you choose what you did? Addressing that will help you grow and make better decisions in the future.*

- *Your circle. The people you surround yourself with can influence your actions. If your environment contributed to this, it's time to rethink who you spend your time with.*

- *Communication. Be honest, vulnerable, and open with her and with yourself.*

- *Seeking help. If you feel like you're struggling with self-control, insecurities, or anything deeper, reaching out to a professional or mentor could make a huge difference. Mind you, speaking from experience. Anyone will tell you how I flipped my whole life around, I kid you not.*

But peep though—you can't pour into someone else's cup when yours is empty. You have to learn to love and respect yourself first. That means working on who you are, not just for her but for you. Whether or not she decides to give you another chance, the work you put in will only make your life better."

Dec 8th

Hey, yes, you've been on my mind today. I miss you because I went to the Natick Mall and drove past the movie theater. All I thought of was that beautiful moment I created for you. I would do it again. I wish the message could get to you, but I want you to get the space you need. Thanks for the good conversation yesterday. Holding you felt amazing, I needed that fr. Damn, another moment just thinking about you, thinking about what you're doing, thinking about how you're feeling, thinking about how I can help you. My situation is different and soon to be better. I am proud of myself and love to see it. I hope we can attend each other's graduation. We really did that shit!!! I started this book called Anxiety, it was one for yours, but I need to use it to cop with what's going on.

Lol, this song really hits different, love, fuck I miss you, baby.

Pnb Rock – Need Somebody

I lied, I fucked called her cause she removed her location on snap!!! I fucking hate this shit!!! I don't want to do this anymore with her!!!

I am not in control anymore, and I am sorry you felt that way. We are always in a balanced relationship where you truly have a voice in whatever we do. If I ever made you feel like we didn't. I apologize truly. I don't want to dominate, I want to conquer with you. I am missing you more today, and I can't face the fact that I am single, and I don't want anyone or anything!!! This shit sucks because I should have listened to you. I should have turned the page on that girl and really focused on what we really have. We have a solid foundation, and it can be built again, but better. You are so strong, and I know you'll be great, but I want to be great with you!!! Baby, you know you wanna come home to me and be great!!

Dec 9th

I want to see you winning, I want to see you okay. I want to see you happy! Whatever that is, I want that for you. You just gotta give it time. Every inch of space is a miracle.

Hey, been thinking about you. I am here at the mall thinking of getting a tattoo. 11:11 is def one of them I wanted to do, even if we don't get back together. That date means so much to me, and it'll forever be stamped. I wish you could know this rn. I'm so excited. I'm missing you, love. I miss you so much. Your touch, your love and your support. I hope you can see the better man in me. I am strong and I am mighty. I fight through anything, and I truly hope you know you have my heart. I am willing to let you go be you. I can't be selfish. I gotta love you from afar, as you are truly healing. Thanks for reminding me how leaving me will make me stronger for anyone. I feel good about the gym. I feel good about myself. I just hope to share it with you. I am not going anywhere until you find you. You deserve the best from me, and I will do that!

Hey love, I am fucking killing this weight rn. I feel good, I want this shit!!! I want to get an 11/11 or 11:11 tat somewhere, idk, on my arm or behind my ear lol, but I'm thinking about it. Lol, what do you think?

Wowwww, the meaning of 11/11 hits so different now. It means the manifestation of a new life/opportunity when I asked for your hand in the engagement, we were asking for a new life and better opportunities. Manifesting that we will be great together. God did say he gives his favorites the toughest battles. Here it is!! I want to learn these things with you. I want to dive deep into what you like and how we can connect on things other than my interests. I don't want this to be a short-term thing. I want this to be a forever thing. You're my best friend. You're my homie. I want you to be a safe haven for me, and I want to be a safe haven for you.

Hey, yes, I wish I could hold you so tight rn. You mean so much to me, and I know you miss me. We need to be together, we need to hold each other through this. I'm tired of being selfish, I'm tired of holding you back. I want to see you grow! Have fun and be the bright, beautiful woman you are. I am sorry I took the dark road to see this, but I really want to be a changed man. I really want you to know that!

Yessssss come get me pls!!! I don't want to be alone anymore.

Dec 10th

Good morning, yes, I hope all is well, and I know you're getting ready to take off for your mini vacation. I woke up this morning feeling so sad. I spent a day without talking to you. A whole day! It was hard, but I gotta keep it going. I don't want to be selfish. I don't want to be unfair. Have a good day!

One day closer to your trip, I hope you have a good time and really enjoy yourself!

Hey, thinking about you today. Just wanna see your face and hold you. I have really been thinking about how much I hurt you and how it can really impact this journey. You are deeply scarred, but over time, wounds will heal themselves with self-love. I hope you find it in you to forgive me and give me another chance.

It's been a hard 24 hours, but I made it through. I didn't text you. I want to reach out to G****, someone other than your mom. I just want to know how you're doing, not where your head is; just genuinely want to know how you're feeling these days. I don't want to bother you, and I'm sure it's just as hard. But you're doing way better than me. I know yo probably angrier than I am. One thing I thought of that makes this person mad is that she can't have my heart like you do. You already won, and the sex doesn't mean anything; although it happened, it just doesn't mean anything to me.

Long work day, and yet I'm still thinking about you. Teaching has been hard, and you're always on my mind when hard to stay focus and talk to the kids. I miss you. Yes, I miss you. Come home, please let me make this right tonight. I am going to pray harder than ever. I am sleeping in my car, cause I just left the gym later than expected and I really can't spend any more money. I know it's tight, but it's what I have to do, damn, this is going to be the greatest story ever, I swear on my life. I disappointed everyone, but I know they're going to love this comeback. I'll be an amazing dad, an amazing person, an amazing partner because this major setback is going to be an incredible comeback. I have a music playlist named The Greatest Comeback Ever. My fuel to fire!!!

Hey Love, I made it for another 24 hours and more. I am Laying in my car at like 1 am. Thinking about my next move. I really want to talk to you about it. I really want to hear from you, but I just think it's so hard not to talk to you, or my life has to get like this. I am sorry, Yes, and I didn't want it to be like this. I need you, and I don't want you to need me!!! I am trying to keep all the negative thoughts away about what you're doing, but it kills me. I am trying to stay pure and focus with no distractions from anyone or anything. That girl has now ghosted me and hasn't talked at all. I deleted all those disgusting pictures and moments I can't believe I took.

Hey love, I'm getting my credit right. I just got a new credit card, and so I'm proud and going to use it appropriately. Living on my own and only me is going to be so much fun and different because I know I'm going to level up for all this. I am waiting to buy stuff for the new place. I need to buy so many cleaning supplies so I can make sure the place is niceeee and clean!! Have a good day, love.

Dec 11th

I can't believe a pet name came up with this girl. I treated this girl like my gf. I feel awful, yet I am happy we are able to better ourselves through this. I really hope to see you at the end. I am trying to make myself stronger mentally and have the capacity to have strong conversations. I am willing to get through whatever you do while you're on your journey. It will be hard, but shit, I'm built for this, and I am willing to do this for you.

WTFFFF I REALLY DID THIS SHITT. I am sorry for not comforting you after this situation. I was mean and nasty. I was also hurt that we are not together anymore. It hit me that we are not on a break. We are not together, and you are a free woman. I can't take it that you may want someone else, but I do know it's going to be hard. I am done cheating. I don't want this shit anymore. I want to be purely in love with you and never see no one else. I felt everything you said, and I really want to put this ring on your finger!!!

YOU CALLED ME TODAY!!!! Omg, I was going to do 72 hours of not talking to you. You don't understand how much I loved that and need that call. You put me on the right track to get my mind right. You truly are someone I want to be with. I am willing to go to the furthest to get us back to where we were and more. You think I'm bluffing, but I am putting in the work, and actions will follow, baby. I swear it will. You're going to get the best version of me!!!! I love you, Yesi, my baby. My love.

Dec 12th

Hey, yes, I just want to say. I can't keep this shit going. You are not allowing me to feel what you feel, and I think it should be a point in time where we both should be able to do that. I want to be there for you, and I want to make you feel heard, but it's hard to keep it just that and more so a stab to the chest when it's not given back, even when it's named. I think I will text you next time I talk to you.

Dec 13th

Yeah, I don't think I want to do this anymore. I want to fully cut you off and just focus on me. I feel like I am just in the middle, and I just don't want to constantly think about if I'm doing too much. I think the fighting stage is over, and it's really about this level up I'm finna do. I am sorry if I'm coming off mean. I just think I'm more than just over the fact of talking here and there, and then giving you space. I just want peace and not be the way I feel like I'm too much. You didn't even want to see me at my low.

Yeah, I feel this way each way I think of it, cause it's like you can do you and have fun, because I think I really solely want to better myself, and not have to worry if you're going to text me or not. I am not trying to say that, but I am telling you this feeling isn't something I want, but I am really feeling it. Something in my mind just allows me to feel that, and I like it cause I am not stressed out or getting upset at anything. You should feel free to do as you please, and so should I. I'm done being selfish, and I am all done with putting limitations on you. I know you want to be a free woman and want to focus on yourself. I ain't mad ut that!

Dec 14th

Hey Love,

I know we are not together, and I know we are trying to figure things out within ourselves, but I want to deeply reflect on my feelings and what I have been going through for the last few days. I truly want to be with you and have high hopes we will get back together. I feel like it is on me to make that happen and make myself the best version of me. I also feel like, with the absence of you and the neglect you've shown me when I was down, it really hurt me to where I thought you loved me, but you couldn't do that. I will go to war with you and do anything that you ask of me. I said I would give you the world, and I still would love to do that. Last night showed how much we love each other, yet we need to figure out what we want to do to get to where we want to go.

As I moved into this new chapter of my life on my own, I truly missed your presence, and it felt as if I would love to celebrate this moment with you. It needs you just as it needs me. Benji needs you; you are my family, and you are my love forever. I love you more and more every day, and it hurts cause I can't give you that. I truly came to realize I am not perfect, but I know I can amazing man for myself and for you.

I kept this note you left me that keeps me grounded, and why I want to make this work. I may lose sight because of high emotions and feelings, but I truly believe you are made for me, and we are made for each other. You deserve better than what I gave you. You deserve more than the world, I want to give you all you ask and mainly loyalty, especially being the only woman in the room I see and want. I feel that shit right now, especially since you are glowing and feeling more and more like yourself. I want no one else but you, and I am holding out on everything/anything to be with you.

No baggage will come with us as we would repair the home we built, but this home is going to be stronger and better. I have big plans for us to make this work again. I think one thing is getting away again and reconnecting with each other, and leaving it all wherever we go. When we return, our same love and clean slate will drive the stronger and beautiful relationship we really have and what we really want. You are valued, you are respected, and you are loved. Please understand, I am not asking you to forgive me yet. I am not asking you to take me back; I am not forcing you to give me anything. I am asking you to hear me out on how we can do this together, just me and me. I am open, I am transparent, I am honest, and I am willing to prove my worth to us, making this work again. You are my rock, you are my better half that I truly need in this life. I did love the messages you sent me as we weren't talking to each other, but I just want to be able to talk to you with emotions cause I fucking care and I love you more than life itself!!! You are my everything!!!! I can't believe someone can have such an impact like that, and I truly will name it that, I CAN'T LIVE LIFE WITHOUT YOU. Yes, I said it, and I do mean that, I fight through this life stuff, but I still try to figure out my life, and it's so empty. Let's figure this out and get through this rough time together and really make us stronger again. I want to say that, and I hope you understand how much you meant to me and how hard I'll fight for you. If you want to talk more about this when you get back, just let me know, love. - Cariño

Dec 18th

Days like this, I feel like you don't want me anymore. You hate me, or there's someone else who has your attention. I feel like I've lost you, and slowly, I wouldn't matter anymore. I hate this feeling, and I know we are going through, but I just don't want to feel like I'm trying for someone and they don't want me. Please know I am not only changing for myself but also for the future that I want to build with you. I am willing to work through anything you want me to because I know how to build something so strong, and sorry I hurt you and destroyed what we built, but now this is a great time for us to build something more beautiful and much stronger than ever. Don't want to lose you, and I don't want to have you around if you don't want to be here. I would love to see you grow, but if it's not for us to do that, I'd have to be the better man and let you go and do that. I know you will be amazing. Idk why I risk that, especially since you've been down for me even more than my whole family. You are my best friend, my forever lover and someone I'd go to war for and with because you have my back like no other. Let me show you how great I can be and truly be the man I want to be and others can admire.

Dec 20th

I didn't get to say it. I felt a lot tho. I think I am ready.

Dec 21st

Today, I feel very strong and ready to let go of Yes. I remember I've been bothering you about an answer and trying to see where you are. I do believe, no answer is an answer. Not saying you are wrong, but this long, we could be having a conversation about next steps, or even if we are done for good. When I say let go, I don't mean that in the wrong way. I want to be with her, and I want to make it work. I need her in my life. I also need a lot of things that I can't have. That's my reality. I am at a place where I am ready to start healing from this breakup officially. No more overthinking if she's going to be with me. No more thinking she's with/talking to someone. I want to choose myself and focus on my self-growth, and I have already seen and felt it over the past month. It's okay to be selfish; it's okay to choose you because I wake up every day with you.

As time goes on, I make my way back to socials, and everything will reset. New page, better me. I promise, I am doing this because this isn't healthy for me to be like this, especially since all I have been doing is giving nothing but space! Space and time are what you ask for. I can't continue to give more time because what about me? That's not fair for me to go through this when you are actually healing (even if you are healing to forgive me) and most likely have your decision.

Again, I am okay with both outcomes. I am ready to let go and let you grow and be with anyone you please. I know you say I am taking the easy way or making it easy for me when we both aren't sure what to feel at times. You are in a better situation and have a better support system, where you seem to be alright. I don't. I want to start because I want to be in a good place in the next month or so. Because I know I met you more than halfway for you to know I want to be better, and I want us to. I exhausted all my options, and I refuse to go back to the insanity. I'm bigger and better than that. I know this better version for me individually, I am going to be better than ever. I am ready to put my head down and grind it outtttt (My Goal is to save at least $10,000 in 6 months). Benji and I are about to be great. I learned so much about myself, and I know I can be the best partner now. I can list all the things, but it's about action. I am ready for a family, I am ready for commitment and ready for my one lady in the room. I felt every emotion, and I couldn't control them. Now, I feel every emotion but yet I can balance and control them. Thank you for telling me everything I need to better myself. I want to take all those and apply them and especially the things I learned. I will never be comfortable, I have never been comfortable cause I am always striving for more and better. Why stop now?? That's my plan. Never be comfortable, go get more.

Dec 22nd

Why do I feel like I am making the wrong decision? Yes, we are broken up, but part of me believes we can still be together, and the other part of me wants to let go. I think it's because you're giving a glimpse of the happiness we both need to be with each other. I am not rushing you or don't want you to resent me, but I do think you need to find out your answer. I truly think that you, as a person you don't need to find that out with another person to realize you want to be with me. That's what I'm scared of, you are trying to seek that through validation, and I don't want that for you. I am saying that cause I am saving myself a little longer to see if we're going to make this work, but I don't want to tell you that, in regards to you know what I am feeling.

The fact that you're waiting out thinking shows you don't want to do this. You're waiting on some sort of action to truly testament your love for me. You believe that saying yes to me would essentially block your blessing. That sounds crazy, the *blessing is that I got my shit together, and I am willing to work it out and fix this with you. That was a hard slap in the face, yet you stood there and still couldn't give me any direction except "I'll respect your decision," like we've been doing this way too long for this to feel like this. If you know, then you know.*

It makes it harder knowing your mom doesn't want us to be together, and it hurts cause I truly loved her as a mom. I really did. It was more of a reason to make me feel like we are not getting back together. I am sorry, yes, but I really think we aren't getting back together, and whatever we decide to do is on us now. No more caring about the other person, it's just what it is.

Dec 23rd

Yes, I made the wrong decision lol, yet it's still in my heart, I want to be with you. Idk how long this can last, but I do know this shit something we need to do to really focus on ourselves. We talked for a good 5 hours, and it felt like we got to a place of clarity. No more talking, no more seeing each other. Straight cold turkey. Idk if I'll feel after this time, but it's going to be so hard. I just hope you don't do what I think you're going to do. So Day 1 is today (12/23/24)

Dec 24th

Here I am, thinking about you hard af. I miss you, and I miss making love to you. The way you ride me and kiss on my neck. You truly make me feel like a king when you're on top of me. I love pleasing you when I'm hitting it from the back and you're feeling every inch of me. I know you don't want to think of me sexually, but baby, you know you're the one I want to be intimate with for now. We have a beautiful bond that just needs to be repaired; some of the things that would make it even better and stronger. I know this time away helps. I hope you realize how your heart wants and needs me.

Fuck you, the moment you said you don't know if you wanna have sex with him. Is my ticket that I can't be with you? You truly think about him, he can have you, cause I ain't nobody's second choice after fun. It's either me or nothing.

I know what I saw last night, and the fact that you didn't want to show me proves me right. I will find out, and if it's true, you're finished. I can't fucking deal with you and how much you lied and all. You are not that person. You are not that way, so you doing this just isn't you.

Last night, you sitting on me felt so good. It was like home, you've been missed at home. I understand, but our love and intimacy are missed, and that connection is what makes us so special. I know I did something wrong to that extent, but it wasn't like it was better, but I always feel something with you, and it's my connection that we are missing rn. I am not saying I want to be intimate now, but I miss you and love you overall.

Our talks are always bad in the beginning cause it's our emotions are high, but in the end, we are calm because we know this is not how we are supposed to be or talk to each other. That's why I don't take it personal or get mad so fast or want to leave on that note cause I know that's not how you feel or nor is that's not how I feel.

Dec 25th

Damn, really woke up on Christmas without you. Shit cuts deep. Yesterday really put into perspective that we need this time away, yet we want to be together. You see me more than the mistake, and the way we go about it isn't healthy for either of us. I want to love you and be

I am fucking shaking rn how much I'm fucking mad and anxious I am. I need to know because that's how I am going to move. I am fucking done thinking we are together. I am going to do me and only myself. Everything will be mine. You'll never see me or anything ever again. Merry Christmas bitch. I fucking hate you, and I know you'll never deserve this better version of me, regardless, cause I know nobody is above me when it comes to who tf I AM.

This is what we came to? Okay, you got this. You wanted this. You will hate me, yes. I will no longer love you no more. I no longer want you to see me anymore.

Dec 26th

I just want to say I don't hate you. I love you more now because you are doing this really forced me to be a better man. I can't believe how many things I am willing to do to get better every day. Day 4 in the gym was pretty good. I called to tell you I love you and not hate you. I know we're not thinking about anything intimate, but I will say I miss your body, I miss your moan, I miss how you ride me, and you're licking and sucking on my neck. You make me feel good, believe it or not. After working out lol you get way more energy and are ready for three rounds. I want to please you so bad, even if that sucking ya toes, how you like it. I love you, yes.

Good night

December 27th

Hey Love, I know this is the day we decided we cannot talk anymore. No more communication, just focusing on us and wanting to be better and healthier than ever.

December 28th

I remember how you made me feel. All my fighting for you was just like "nigga leave me tf alone" type of voice, and I really thought we could get somewhere together. You want to be alone and on your own makes me think you want to seek other things, which is fine. I just can't deal with not knowing what tf we are doing. I think I'll delete you, and once I figure out when I come back on IG.

December 29th

Hey love. I miss you, and it's only been one day. Let's make it a week, the stronger the better. I'll be missing you more and more every day. I am staying strong for the hope that we can get there. I want to write in that little book that describes everything I love about you, and I will find and know every single thing I love about you. I am also going to write you a letter, just mail it to you and so you can see and read how I am feeling, even texting you. You don't have to write back; you just have to read. That's it. I hope that's okay. I love you, yes, and just being around my friends like Manny and Kay makes me more fond of missing you fr. You're my best friend, and we do everything together. I want it to be like forever. You're my bestie, and I need you back in my life. I love you again.

Dec 30th

I fucking hate you!!! You are the worst, and you make me feel like shit!!!

Dec 31st

Same shit, different day. We need space to get over this breakup, and no one besides 2G is answering me. Thanks, bro, I appreciate you, twin.

January 1st

This is why I delete social media fr.

Hey, yes, I spoke to **** and it really gave some clarity on what I need to do moving forward. I will let you go and grow into being the better you, even if it's not for me. Thanks again for pushing me to be my best self, cause lord knows this is what I need. As I said, I wasn't all in, and I need to learn that the hard way. I feel more at peace that we are doing this to better ourselves. No contact should have been started after the breakup up but it's so hard when you love someone. I will not close my heart to you because my heart does want you, and try to make this right again on better terms. I made a goal for myself this year, and I am going to be super hard on myself cause this is the year I'll be golden and reach the potential I'm supposed to hit.

Going through my notes and reading every time I hurt you, praise you, and love you. It sometimes feels like I was lying because of the actions I did, but I know for a fact I love and care for you, yes. I truly do think this is for us to come back stronger than ever because we do have great chemistry and ppl can see that too. I know I hurt, and now I am hurt cause I am losing you. I love you so much it hurts. I can't help you, and I caused this. I will be better, and I know I will. I am glad I wrote down my notes so far. Twenty-four hours have passed since we talked. Let's keep it going.

Jan 2nd

24hrs down… damn this shit is hard. I miss you, love, wyd? How was your day? What's ya plan for the evening?

I hope to be able to take you out after at least these 30 days of not speaking should help calibrate our relationship and how much we may miss each other.

Jan 3rd

While I was chatting with Jean, he sent me this: "So MAKE THIS THE FUCKING LAST TIME you ever hurt her or anyone else," all cause I was tripping out of not talking to you. He snapped me back to reality. I needed that. Anyway, how was your day? You work? I miss you so much, yes. I went on my iPad, and I literally was in a funk cause the cute pics we took at my Halloween party. You looked so good, and I remember I was drunk afffff lol but what a night it was, baby. I wish I could hold you rn. Sleeping alone is not fun, especially since you've been my baby I slept with the last 6 years. I wish I could have that rn. I try to get my 11:11 tattoo, but no one can do it at a decent price fr!!! But I know my journey, I am heading on the right path, and I love the new things I am doing fr. Thank you! Well, you get some rest cause I have nothing else to do rn either. Been working a lot fr. I wanna hit that 10k fr. Maybe invest in your studio.. Couldn't sleep; all I thought of was you. I feel like today gonna be hard, but we can do this fr

Here I am at the laundry Mat cleaning my clothes lol lowkey feel like a big boy cause man I had so many clothes. This laundry smells so good lol confidence on a 1000. This living on my own has had its time, but this is nothing new to me. This is just hard cause I feel alone even with Benji lol. My friends come by all but just not the same when I get up, and you're not next to me fr. I am keeping hope alive, but I believe you'll be back cause you know I will be better than ever, and I love you more than life itself.

Damn love, this is the first time I am watching a movie without you and shit, this is so harddddd like fr. This is truly our thing!!! Why did I have to fuck this shit up like ya mom said? I fucked a lot in my life, but this one felt and is the biggest fuck up. I lost a lot and gained so little. I mean, from what I am feeling now. I think I'll see how great I am after the 30 days of not talking to you. These notes shit help cause I could've easily called you Yes. Hope you had a good day or week of work. Have some fun this weekend to get over the 1st week jitters!!

Lol, I just ate, and you know what happens after I eat. Damn, I wanna be in you rn. Loving you and touching you. Sucking ya nipples and holding ya waist when you're riding me. Omg this is making me too horny rn to be thinking about this baby. Come

Home, come hold me and lemme embrace your love again.

72 Hours down 672 Hours left… keep going, don't stop. You are worth it, and you can do it.

Omg, today was so harddddd, I felt so horny for you and only you. And I know if I had this feeling…it's not going to feel good after with someone else. That post nut clarity shit is real, and I know I'll feel bad. It's not you, and it's not the way to go.

I wish I were ending my night with you, Yesi. Shittttt

Jan 5th

96 hours of no contact… wtffff 4 days!!!!! This will become easier. You think I'll love you less and less? I am afraid I am coming into form and being active a bit on social media. I hope this doesn't change how I feel about you.

We have a conversation in 2 weeks, maybe a month? Idk

Why do I have a feeling you are talking to someone, regardless of you saying you *don't want anyone?? You're saying you want to be by yourself, yet you're probably entertaining someone right now. Just fucking tell me you don't want to be with me. Okay, yes, you can't be with me right now, but in reality, you fucking know. We can get past this regardless of the outcome, but I need to start removing shit.*

Yesterday I missed you, today I just don't think we can or want to be together. I say this cause the mixed feelings of whether we are going to make this work or not. Shits annoying and I am not patience enough to know if I'm going to be with the love of my life yet. I pray we at least get an answer; it doesn't matter which way. I just want to know so we can move on already.

Went on a solo date for the 1st time. It was pretty cool. Met an old couple and a family of 4 while I was out lol it felt weird cause I wanted both with you. A family and grow old with you. Overall great experience, next step is the movies lol this one gonna be super hard fr but this is me finding myself again and I like it and it's a lot cheaper.

Jan 6th

Today I realize if I own what I did and truly accept that mistake, I can now understand and accept the actions and what you decided to do is fair 1000%. You need space to process what happened, essentially heal from the pain I endured, and how I really ruined and destroyed the beautiful thing we built. I hurt you deeply, where you may think men in your life are just going to come and go. Not this man. You are learning to forgive me, or at least that's a part of the process. I trust your heart and mind will be aligned to make the decision you truly feel. All I can do is respect the space and love you from afar. As for me...I will focus on getting better and healing from this wound as well. I have more days that I love you than days when I hate you. I feel that way cause I wouldn't be this much into myself to fix the issues to make me an almost perfect man. Today, I love you, and I actually do appreciate you. You definitely put me in a position to find who I really am again. I am someone who never settles or gets comfortable because I strive for so much more in and this time around, I've been through so much. I don't need the validation because I know how great I am, and I don't need that from someone else. I've seen more growth in this short period of time than I ever did in my life. I can damn well say I am proud of myself. I want to continue to be proud and be the man I forever want to be today, tomorrow and eternity.

Jan 7th

I feel eh, but I don't feel good. I feel like I keep running into the same thing every time I speak to yes, and she doesn't get it. It's fine, I'll be better for sure.

Jan 9th

I feel good today, didn't think much about her until she texted the notes app we have and reminded me how much fun we're having. Thanks for the reminders, don't want to keep getting them. I'll regress for sure lol.

Jan 11th

Days like this, wanting to talk to them are getting thinner and thinner. Hope you like this.

The moment you do something, I know you're trying to contact me or know or post a memory…I'm getting you outta here.

I do realize that as time goes by, the decision I make isn't about what I want to do. It's really about trying to hurt her because of what she's doing to me. This isn't the man I want to be. I want to be bigger and better than that, and trying to hurt her doesn't help our situation if I want to be with her. My hurt to her is temporary, and she will eventually get over it. I should make her feel like she's worthy and she deserves this time, and also deserves a better me. So, trying to delete our photos and remove her from socials isn't something that can help, and I can't see myself doing it anyway. I think we should sit and talk about it like we always have, especially when we see each other.

Jan 12th

Unfollow me cause I came back on IG lol.

Jan 13th

I am starting to feel like I don't need or want anyone rn. Even yes. No woman for some time, and I truly want to go on a trip on my own. Just me or the girls? It'll be our first getaway. That would be cool.

Feb 16th

damn, I have been here since Jan 13th. This transition has been difficult but yet manageable. Today I see you, and you're looking stunning. My beautiful lady, you shining girl lol have ya moment talk to shit I'm rooting for you from afar. You got this! Now back to the grindddddddd lol

Feb 18th

Wow, we are actually communicating, but on a very healthy level. No fast replies, not lovie dovie!! We are being what we imagine we can do. I am taking her out on Saturday.

Feb 19th

I didn't fall for you because I needed a relationship; I fell for you because, for the first time in forever felt at peace, and you made me feel loved, and you never judged me. I just let my ego and my accomplishments make me stagnant and comfortable, the root of the bad decisions, lack of communication and most importantly, my love and respect for our beautiful relationship.

I am very nervous about it because I don't know what to expect. I want to feel every motion so I can know what to do and how to make it better for myself. This ain't gonna be a short drive to Chick-fil-A or something, it is more so we're spending the day with each other. Who knows what may come outta this? Maybe we want to see what we feel like if we have a spark between us again. If it's the same or better.

I don't want any distractions, no worries and just want to be in the moment with you. I think it may get spontaneous, and we just stay in Framingham, and I am okay with it. I certainly will be okay with no sex. I am moving with her; she leads, I follow and respect.

March 6

The date went well, we felt all the right things, and we want this, but we need time still to get better and through this.

March 16th

I think I did something I wasn't supposed to. I did the tat thing, and I think I either spoiled it too early or I did it too early. I really think I should have waited to either show or tell. I'm lowkey having regrets, yet I still think I am doing what I want to do and what feels right to me. What makes me feel this way is that I need to understand we are two different times and that maybe I am not supposed to be at this point with her, and she's supposed to be doing her own. I think I am going to fall back, and even if we lose our snap streak, I'm cool with just giving the space. Let me give this the 24, 48, 72 rule, and I will come back with my thoughts.

March 27th

Today made me realize how much you love life without me. You and your family are doing well, and don't think twice about me entering your life again. Do I think I was just making a pit stop and making my way to something different? Are we both not for each It was just a phase. I don't want to believe it, but I think that's what I am feeling. When you feel like you've exhausted yourself trying to be there for someone, you really think about yourself and realize you are losing yourself. I know what I did with the Tat, and I honestly feel like it was to show how serious I was and how much you mean to me. Although I wanted to do it, I really think it was too early, but I still wouldn't regret it. I love you and will always love you. That's all I am going to say. Until then, be safe and be great.

March 28th

We are going to try and be together, we want this and want each other.

April 7th

She ruined me

April 9th

Why did you hurt me like this??? All I have done to get back to a place of peace and strength, I can't eat, I can't sleep haven't even left my house. Can't even touch my bed; I haven't showered. I'm a wreck because of this. I get it, you want to focus on yourself and eventually move on. Glad you made the decision. This shit is eating my soul to where I can't even function anymore. Benji is sitting here just watching me suffer this pain and agony. My therapist can't even get to me because I'm too emotional. These last two days have been hell. I respect that you want to pour for yourself, but I wasn't asking for too much anyway. I wanted us to solely be there for each other, and again let you grow on your own. I knew the moments I named my non-negotiable, you were already one foot out, but whatever you needed, I was willing to give it. We had no chance at this because it was cut before it even started. I came back from hard shit, but this is different. The amount of love and energy I poured into this rebuild for it to get knocked down. I want to be evil so bad towards you, I really do, but I can't because I seee you as my wife and someone I have forever wanted to be with. I made promises now that I can't keep, and I truly destroyed something so beautiful. Idk how you are, but this shit really cut me deep. I'm so fucking devastated, I don't even wanna face anything or anyone. Just get me out of here so I can start over.

May 2nd

I am only saying this because I want to break the no contact rule because I am feeling better than before. I am living like there is no return. I am not thinking about getting back together anymore. Once my therapist said, "There is No Contact', it's just over". In reality, we are our own individuals who are ready to work on ourselves or to be with someone. I do think I am ready to move on. All these situations have been suppressed at least on my side. I think the damage to you, your family & friends I caused will be difficult to come back from, and chances are very slim. As I was so in love with you, I was willing to go all out. Turns out I did that, and it hurt me more than ever. I don't feel anything, as much as I thought I would, especially how everything went down. I fucked up badly to the point I don't even want to return. I gave so much I can't even give anymore. I feel like I am speaking for today and forever. I think the chapter of Yesi and Jay is completely over, and I truly think that since we tried (technically), I feel like we have nothing to give regardless. Instead of you saying it, I am completely moving on, and I want you to know that. I don't want to hurt you and nor want you to think anything of this. I just want us to completely understand what we know is going to happen, at least for me. Thanks for making me realize I had to get my shit together and become a man. I thought it would take years, instead it took me alone time to finally feel and be the man I want to be right now (thinking about my future, finances, self-discipline and most importantly my physical and mental health.)

Overall, I don't have any hate for you. I just think no point in hanging around more. I will coordinate with mom about the computer, the monitor and the storage unit. With love Jay

May 5th

I can't believe this, but I am missing you more than you think. I am so torn, and I truly believe we are each other's 1s. I can't stop thinking about you and loving you from afar. Every day, I am waiting by my phone for your call or text. I want to hear your voice, I want to hold you more than anything. I really need you, yes. I am dying slowly.

June 22nd

Today she officially blocked me on all socials, I have no contact of texting her or see her page on whatever social media.

June 25th

I think it really hit me today. I needed this separation completely. I have a clear mind, and I really needed to get myself together this is in every aspect. I think one day I'd thank her, but it'll never be something I'll do. If it happens, then so be it. Other than that, she'll never hear from me again.

Epilogue, The Man I'm Becoming

June 25th was the day I decided enough was enough.
Not with her. Not with the past. But with the version of myself that kept breaking what he prayed for.
That was the day I stopped writing for her and started writing for me.
The journal ended there—but my rebuilding began.

Every entry before that captured a man trying to make sense of loss. But after that day, I started living for something bigger than closure. I wanted peace, purpose, and the kind of growth you can't fake. That's when I told myself, *if I'm going to be rebuilt, it has to be from the ground up.*

That's why this epilogue isn't about an ending—it's about a beginning. Because the man I'm becoming didn't rise overnight. He was shaped one prayer, one page, one choice at a time.

You're probably wondering what I'm up to now.

Truth is, I'm still becoming. Still growing. Still learning how to live in the peace I used to pray for.

These days, it's just me and my roommate, Benji. He's been with me through every version of myself: the broken, the rebuilding, and the reborn. We've created our own rhythm—early mornings, late nights, quiet drives, and plenty of laughter in between. Life feels steady now. Purposeful. I'm teaching and coaching basketball at a new school, and every day feels like another step toward the man I was meant to be.

Coaching has turned into more than a job—it's a calling. Every time I step into the gym and hear "Let's go, Coach Jay!", something in me comes alive. The court has become my sanctuary, a place where lessons about the game turn into lessons about life. I've realized you can teach so much more than basketball—you can teach patience, respect, and brotherhood. You can teach how to lead when emotions run high and how to stand tall after a loss. My mindset isn't just to raise great players, but to help build great people.

I tell my kids often: *basketball is the common ground, but character is what carries you through life.* And in teaching them, they've taught me too. They've reminded me that purpose doesn't always announce itself—it shows up quietly, disguised as the thing you've loved since you were young.

The transition into single life wasn't easy. There's a kind of silence that hits when the future you imagined fades away. That silence used to scare me. It felt like punishment. But over time, I realized it was preparation—God's way of slowing me down so I could finally listen.

At first, I tried to fill that silence with distractions. I posted more. I reached out when I shouldn't have. I pretended to be fine when I wasn't. But healing doesn't live in noise—it lives in the quiet. So, I stepped back. I locked in at the gym. I deleted social media. I sat with my emotions, even the ones I didn't want to face.

Some days, I missed love. Other days, I wanted nothing to do with it. But every emotion had a purpose. The sadness, the anger, the loneliness—they were all teachers. They showed me who I really was when no one else was watching.

I still attend therapy, and I'm proud of that. Therapy didn't fix me—it freed me. It gave me language for the feelings I used to bury and helped me understand that healing isn't about returning to who you were; it's about growing into who you're meant to be. It's my tune-up, my mirror, my accountability. I've learned that mental health is part of the foundation, and I'm building mine brick by brick.

My family has been my anchor through it all.

My mom—my rock. Even as she fights her own battles behind closed doors, she still finds joy in watching me evolve. I'll never forget when she said, *"You're just like your dad, but better."* Those words hit deep. Thank you, Momma. I love you endlessly. Your strength has always been my blueprint.

And Nana—my queen, my forever muse. Whether it's a new iPad or your favorite bag of classic Lay's chips, you always get what you ask for. You and Mom have been my foundation—the two women who held me together when I could've fallen apart. You are the heartbeat of this story. Your love made me whole again.

And then there's God. He's been there through every silent night, every small victory, every whispered prayer. I talk to Him every day—not out of routine, but out of gratitude. He helped me rebuild my faith and, in doing so, reconnected me to my dad. There are moments when I feel my father's presence, like he's watching me, guiding me, and nodding in approval. That feeling makes me whole again. I spent years searching for the missing piece, only to realize it was a connection to God, to my roots, to myself.

Now, as I work toward completing my Doctorate in Sports Leadership, I'm in a place where I'm constantly challenged to expand my thinking—not just in my career, but in every area of my life. It's pushing me to see leadership beyond titles and achievements. It's teaching me to serve with purpose and vision. And I'm grateful I chose to do this now, before I start a family—because the goal is to build the foundation first. To be prepared for what's next, not just hope I can handle it when it comes.

The dream is still alive—to one day work for the Boston Celtics. That's the kid in me still chasing the impossible, doing it for the city that raised him. But more than that, I want to use my story, my education, and my platform to inspire—to show others that pain doesn't end your story; it refocuses it.

I've learned that healing isn't a race. It's not about proving who's happier or who moved on faster. Healing is between you and God. It's written in silence, growth, and faith.

And I'll always respect her for choosing herself, even when it meant breaking my heart, because that moment forced me to meet myself. That's when I knew I had finally stepped into the man I was meant to become.

These days, I sleep peacefully. No guilt. No replaying the past. I'm not perfect, but I'm proud. I've forgiven, I've released, and I've come home to myself.

And when love finds me again—and I know it will—I'll be ready. Ready to love with peace, not pain. With trust, not fear. With purpose, not ego.

I'm not rushing it. I'm not chasing it. I'm just becoming the kind of man who can hold it the right way when it arrives. I have hope that with the right energy, mindset, and heart, I'll attract someone special—someone I can grow and ride through life with.

I stopped searching for revenge or validation.

I found peace instead—and that's the real win.

Before You Go

(For Every Soul Reading)

"Wow… Jay and Yes aren't together anymore."

That's what people probably said when they found out. And that's fine, because that night in December, the 10th, sitting alone in the parking lot long after midnight, I already knew my story was about to become something special.

That was the moment it all began. The moment I felt something shift inside me. I remember sitting there, quiet, heart heavy, but something in me whispering that there was purpose in the pain. I spoke it into existence that night and prayed for it. I didn't know what form it would take, but I knew I had to turn what broke me into something that could build me.

My phone was filled with everything I couldn't say out loud, words to her, to myself, to God. Every emotion, every regret, every truth that hurt too much to speak lived in that notes app. I wasn't writing for sympathy or attention. I was writing because silence was killing me, and I needed somewhere to put the weight I was carrying.

When my therapist asked one day, "How have you been expressing yourself through all this?" I handed her my phone. She scrolled through my notes and just stared at me, shocked.

She said, "You turned your pain into poetry."

But I didn't see it that way. I wasn't trying to be poetic, I was trying to survive. I just wanted to say what I felt, to be honest about the mess, the mistakes, and the man underneath it all.

From that December night forward, I wrote almost every day. I wrote when I couldn't sleep. I wrote through the anger, the confusion, the heartbreak. I wrote while trying to process the fear of possibly losing my mom, the strongest woman I know, and at the same time, trying to forgive myself for the man I used to be.

The woman guiding me through therapy told me something I'll never forget:

"Let the people hear you. Let them feel that you're sorry. Don't just say it, show it. Put them in front of you and let them feel the man you've worked hard to become."

That's what this book became, not an apology in words, but an apology in action—a mirror of accountability, growth, and grace.

This project has been a **year-long process**, a year of reflection, rebuilding, and release. I've rewritten, re-read, and relived some of the hardest moments of my life, but I've also found new peace, new faith, and a new sense of purpose. I plan to release this book on **December 1st**, my birthday, because it represents exactly that: rebirth. Not just another year of life, but a better way of living it.

My mom's strength pushed me to become the man she always saw in me. I couldn't let her leave this world without seeing her son stand tall again. And my Nana, my queen, she's my constant reminder that love never stops giving. Their love, their prayers, and their faith in me brought me back to myself.

And God, He's been here through every second of it. I talk to Him every day. I know He helped me reconnect with my father in spirit, to feel his presence guiding me, to remind me that nothing I lost was wasted. Every test was a preparation. Every scar was an instruction.

This isn't me asking for sympathy.

This isn't about victimizing myself or proving who healed first. I'm not here to compare stories or keep score; that's not what growth looks like.

This is my healing, and this is what it looks like.

It's been late nights of reflection, early mornings in prayer, therapy sessions that made me face my own reflection, workouts that cleared my head, and days of silence that taught me how to listen to my soul. Healing isn't glamorous. It's raw, it's slow, and it's honest. It's learning to show up when no one's clapping for you. It's forgiving yourself again and again until it sticks.

I'm not perfect. I'm not finished. But I'm committed.

Healing for me isn't about racing to a finish line; it's about showing up every day with intention.

It's in the way I coach, the way I love, the way I speak, and the way I protect my peace.

If there's anything I want you to take from this book, it's that healing is humble work. It's quiet, lonely at times, but it's real. It's not about who sees you, it's about who you become when no one does. I didn't write this to make anyone look bad. I wrote this so people could see that it's possible to grow, to change, and to choose love again without fear.

This book isn't about the pain; it's about the promise that came from it. It's about a man who finally decided to face himself, forgive himself, and free himself.

The man in these pages still lives, but now he moves differently. He's learned to love without conditions, to walk without pretending, and to stand without guilt. He's learned that peace doesn't need to be proven; it just needs to be protected.

If you've ever been broken, doubted, or misunderstood, I hope my story shows you this:

Your healing won't look like mine, but it will be worth it.

Because pain might start your story, but it doesn't get to finish it.

Thank you for reading mine.

Now it's your turn to write yours.

Jaiwaun Haggerty

"I'm no longer running from the man I was. I'm walking with the one I became."